Rainforest

Published in Great Britain in MMXIV by
Book House, an imprint of
The Salariya Book Company Ltd
25 Marlborough Place, Brighton BN1 1UB
www.salariya.com
www.book-house.co.uk

PB ISBN-13: 978-1-909645-76-9

S A L A R I Y A

1 3 5 7 9 8 6 4 2

A CIP catalogue record for this book is available
from the British Library.

Printed and bound in China.

Visit our website at **www.book-house.co.uk**
or go to **www.salariya.com** for **free** electronic versions of:
You Wouldn't Want to be an Egyptian Mummy!
You Wouldn't Want to be a Roman Gladiator!
You Wouldn't Want to be a Polar Explorer!
You Wouldn't Want to sail on a 19th-Century Whaling Ship!

Visit
www.salariya.com
for our online catalogue and **free**
interactive web books.

A CLOSER LOOK AT

Rainforest

Written by Margot Channing
Illustrated by Carolyn Scrace

CONTENTS

A rainforest is a complicated ecological system. It is made up of several layers of plants and trees, each playing an important part in the rainforest habitat. Each layer consists of different plants and trees, and the animals that live in them.

The rainforest is also home to the people who live in it. Humans have lived in the rainforests for hundreds of years.

SAVING RAINFORESTS

Rainforests are treasure troves of a vast array of species. Many rainforest plants and animals are still not fully understood and it is highly likely that many more have yet to be discovered. To conservationists, saving the Earth's rainforests from destruction is one of the most important challenges facing the world today.

Butterfly

Scientists have discovered many wonderful rainforest creatures, such as poison dart frogs and butterflies. However, there are probably still many creatures yet to be found.

Poison dart frog

This book takes a closer look at the Earth's rainforests, from the giant trees that grow there to the animals that live on the forest floor and in its magnificent rainforest rivers.

Harpy eagle

Common squirrel monkey

IN THE TREE TOPS

The branches and trees that grow around 30 – 40 m above the rainforest floor are called the 'canopy'. Some canopy trees have huge leaves that can grow up to 6 m long. Most rainforest animals live in the canopy, where they can easily find shelter and plenty to eat.

Toucan

WATER WORLD

More than 6,000 mm of rainwater falls on the rainforest each year. The canopy catches at least 80 per cent of this water. Only 20 per cent of the rainfall reaches the forest floor.

Rainforest monkeys swing from branch to branch in the canopy, looking for food. Colourful birds also dart among the leaves of the tree tops.

Red-faced ukari

HANGING AROUND

Sloths are rainforest animals. They spend much of their lives in the canopy. Sloths hang upside down, clinging to branches with their strong claws. They are so used to hanging upside down that they even give birth to their babies in this position!

Sloth

Butterfly

TREE TRUNKS

High above the rainforest floor, orchids, mosses and ferns grow on the giant tree trunks. Soil-filled cracks in the tree trunks provide a home for creatures such as worms. Water collects in the tree bark or in cup-shaped bromeliad plants. The water forms drinking pools and little ponds where frogs lay their eggs.

ANTS AND WASPS

Leaf-cutter ants chew off pieces of leaves and carry them to their underground nests. There, the leaves rot into fungus, which the ants feed to their babies. Wasps chew up wood from the tree trunks to turn into material for building their nests.

Ants

Wasp

Tent-making bats fold leaves in half to make a dry shelter for their young.

PRICKLY PORCUPINE

Porcupines live on rainforest trees. These prickly creatures are covered in sharp spines to deter predators. They also have prehensile tails, which they use like an extra hand to grip onto twigs and branches.

Tree porcupine

Mosses

Bromeliad

SHRUBS AND SMALL TREES

Tall shrubs and trees of less than 10 m in height make up the rainforest 'understorey'. The trees of the understorey are usually young ones that have been unable to grow taller because they do not have enough sunlight. When one of the forest's giant trees dies and falls down, sunlight finally reaches the smaller trees, which then get a chance to grow taller.

CREEPING CREEPERS

The glossy green leaves of many understorey creepers are so pretty that people keep them as houseplants.

Common squirrel monkey

Night monkey

Night monkeys have big brown eyes. They sleep during the day and are awake at night, which is when they look for food, such as insects.

MOSSY WORLD

In the damp, dark world of the understorey, mosses and algae grow. They are found on tree trunks, creepers and even on some animals! Some sloths turn green, coloured by algae growing on their fur.

IN THE SHADE

Deep beneath the canopy and understorey of the rainforest, it is shady. There, little vegetation grows. Only plants that do not need much light, such as mosses and ferns, survive. While the damp and shade does not suit many plants, it suits predators. The shady parts of the rainforest are their hunting ground.

Jaguar

DEADLY CATS

Jaguars lurk in the bushes and climb the low branches. They lie in wait for prey. These animals are coloured fawn and brown, which helps them to hide in the undergrowth.

Chicks

Woolly opposum

SKILFUL SNAKES

Rainforest snakes are skilful hunters. They glide silently along the forest branches to catch roosting birds or steal the eggs from their nests.

Snake

Many snakes are brightly patterned. Their strong colouring warns off any creatures that might try to attack them.

The soil of the rainforest floor is thin and stony. Only the rotting plants and dead animals that litter the forest floor contain nutrients. Fallen trees, plants and animal corpses rot in the damp warmth of the rainforest floor. As they rot, they create a layer of material called 'humus'.

POISONOUS FROG

Poison arrow frogs live on the rainforest floor. They produce a poison, called venom, in the glands beneath their skin. One frog species, the golden arrow frog, produces the deadliest poison ever discovered.

Litter frog

Poison arrow frog

CREEPY-CRAWLIES

On the forest floor, ants and termites make nests from the crumbly soil. Thousands of insects and other creepy-crawlies live among the fallen leaves and rotting wood of the forest floor.

Beetle

Ants

The nightjar bird feeds on insects at night. The bird has huge eyes that help it to see in the dark.

Nightjar

IN THE JUNGLE

In the forest clearings and by the riverbanks, patches of jungle grow. Jungle is made up of ferns, saplings, vines and other creepers. These plants twist together to form a thick wall that is almost impossible to cut through.

Chameleons catch flies with a flick of the tongue.

Spider

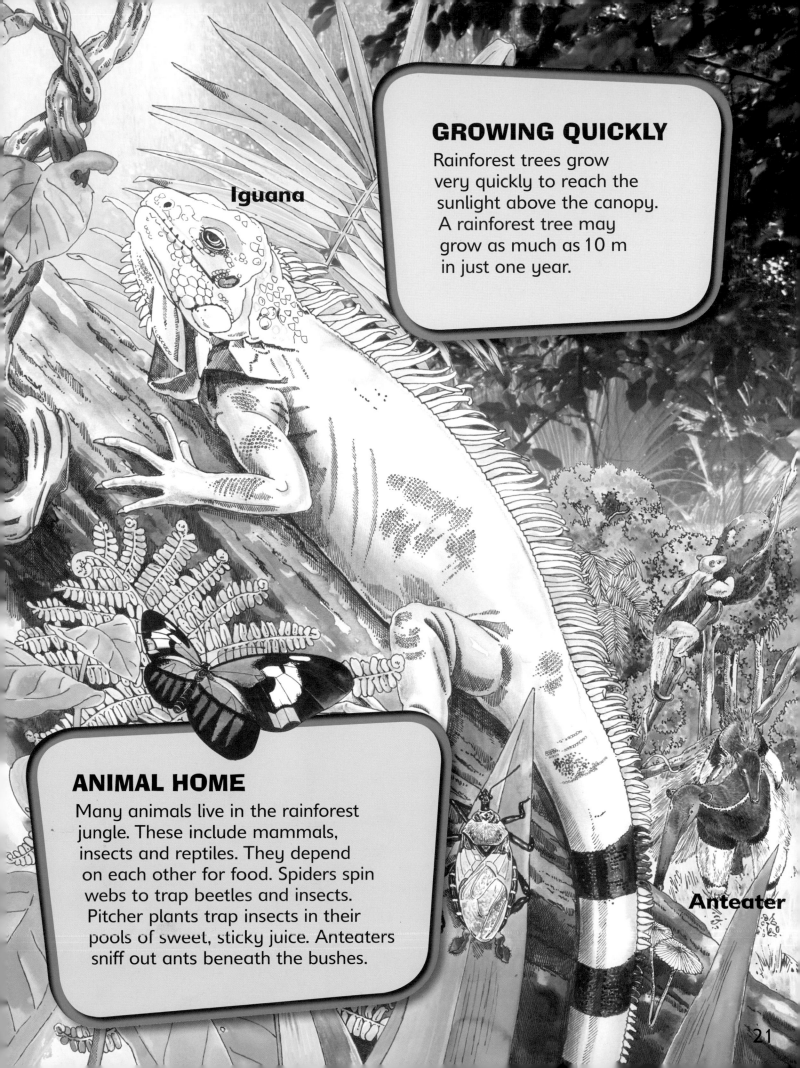

Iguana

GROWING QUICKLY

Rainforest trees grow very quickly to reach the sunlight above the canopy. A rainforest tree may grow as much as 10 m in just one year.

ANIMAL HOME

Many animals live in the rainforest jungle. These include mammals, insects and reptiles. They depend on each other for food. Spiders spin webs to trap beetles and insects. Pitcher plants trap insects in their pools of sweet, sticky juice. Anteaters sniff out ants beneath the bushes.

Anteater

THE RIVERBANK

The thick roots and fresh green shoots of many rainforest plants form clumps and thickets that line the riverbank. Many reptiles and amphibians live in this warm, damp, sunny layer of the forest. Snakes, frogs, toads and terrapins bask in the sunshine, then slip into the cool river water in search of food.

RIVERSIDE DRINKER

Cabybaras are relatives of guinea pigs, but they are much bigger. These animals can grow up to 1.3 m long. They live along the riverbank.

Cabybara

The baby hoatzin bird uses the claws on its wings to cling onto rainforest branches. If it needs to escape from predators, it quickly lets go and drops into the river below.

Baby hoatzin

OTTERS IN DANGER

Giant otters live in the rainforest rivers. Unfortunately, these creatures are becoming rare because they are hunted for their thick, glossy fur.

Giant otter

IN THE RIVER

Many rainforest creatures live in the swirling waters of the river below. The huge Amazon River is more than 6,400 km long and travels from the snowy Andes Mountains to the ocean. It is so deep that ships can sail upriver from the ocean for more than half the river's length!

Flesh-eating piranhas live in the Amazon River. These deadly fish devour any animals that fall into the water.

Dolphin

RIVER SWIMMERS

The Amazon River is home to more than 1,500 species of fish. These include angel fish, hatchet fish and discus fish. Stingrays also swim in the Amazon River, as do freshwater dolphins.

DEADLY CRUSH

Anaconda snakes live in the Amazon River. These giant snakes can grow up to 9 m in length and are one of the largest creatures in the rainforest. Anacondas feed on animals as large as caiman. The snake kills its prey by wrapping its long body around it before crushing it to death. The snake then eats its prey.

Caiman

Anaconda

Stingray

Angel fish

25

For hundreds of years, the people of the rainforest have lived there without harming the environment. Their way of living may seem very primitive to people in modern cities. However, rainforest people have learned how to feed, house, clothe and cure themselves from illness using only the forest and its produce.

Rainforest village

Locally grown food

GROWING FOOD

People of the rainforest clear small areas of the forest to build houses and grow crops. After a few years, when the soil no longer sustains farming, they move on to a new area of the rainforest. The area they abandon will soon revert into rainforest once more.

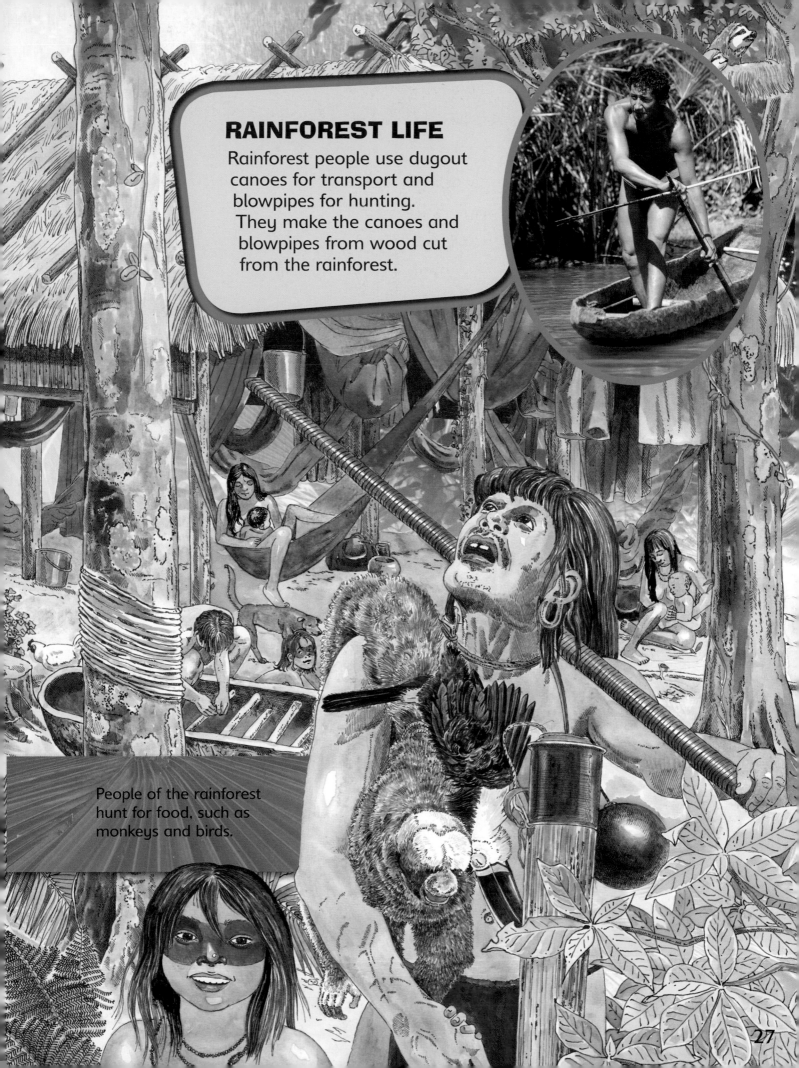

RAINFOREST LIFE

Rainforest people use dugout canoes for transport and blowpipes for hunting. They make the canoes and blowpipes from wood cut from the rainforest.

People of the rainforest hunt for food, such as monkeys and birds.

RAINFOREST UNDER THREAT

The rainforests are being cut down for their timber and to make room for ranches, mines and plantations. This is called 'deforestation'. Every year, an area of rainforest the size of England is destroyed. If we keep destroying the rainforest at this rate, the consequences for the whole of the planet will be severe. Rainforests are precious and we need to do all we can to protect them.

Deforestation

AN IMPORTANT SPONGE

A rainforest acts like a sponge, soaking up any water that falls on it. When the forest is cut down, the rainwater runs off the land, carrying the rich topsoil with it. The soil that remains has so few nutrients that little can grow in it. The topsoil that is washed away runs into the rivers, which burst their banks and then flood the land around them.

GREENHOUSE DANGER

Forests absorb a lot of carbon dioxide. This is a gas that is present in the air. When carbon dioxide builds up in the atmosphere, it traps the sun's heat. This causes the Earth's surface to warm up. This is known as the 'greenhouse effect'. The greenhouse effect will get worse unless we stop chopping down the rainforest.

Atmosphere

The rainforest is being cleared each year to make room for livestock farming. Trees are also cut down for wood.

GLOSSARY

Algae very simple plants that are made up of one cell or chains of cells. Algae live in water or on damp surfaces.

Blowpipe a hollowed-out stick that rainforest people use for hunting. Hunters blow down the pipe to shoot a dart forward.

Bromeliad a plant of the pineapple family, usually with stiff, leathery leaves.

Canopy the thick layer of vegetation that forms the 'roof' of the rainforest.

Dugout canoe a boat made from a single, hollowed-out tree trunk. The wood is chopped out by axes or burned away by fire.

Ecological to do with animals and plants.

Environment the surroundings where plants, animals or people live.

Fungus plant-like organisms that cannot make their own food, as most plants do.

Gland a part of the body. Glands produce chemicals that the body needs, sometimes for defence.

Humus loose, soft soil that is made up of decayed plant and animal matter.

Insect a small animal with six legs, two or four wings and a body divided into three sections.

Nutrients important parts of food, such as vitamins and minerals.

Plantation specially cleared land where plants, such as bananas, are grown. Carefully managed plantations do not harm rainforests. Badly run plantations can destroy them forever.

Predator an animal that hunts and eats other animals.

Prehensile capable of grasping things.

Ranch a large farm where vast numbers of cattle usually roam free over wide open spaces. Cattle ranchers have to cut down huge areas of rainforest to make room for their cattle to roam. This has caused serious damage to the rainforests of South America.

Species a group of animals or plants that is different from all other groups.

Understorey the middle layer of the rainforest that is beneath the canopy and above the forest floor.

Venom poison produced by an animal.

Vine a plant with a long stem that grows along the ground or wraps itself around tree trunks.

INDEX